Welcome to Brazil

by Alison Auch

Content and Reading Adviser: Mary Beth Fletcher, Ed.D.
Educational Consultant/Reading Specialist
The Carroll School, Lincoln, Massachusetts

Spyglass
BOOKS

COMPASS POINT BOOKS

Minneapolis, Minnesota

Compass Point Books
3722 West 50th Street, #115
Minneapolis, MN 55410

Visit Compass Point Books on the Internet at *www.compasspointbooks.com*
or e-mail your request to *custserv@compasspointbooks.com*

Photographs ©: PhotoDisc, cover, 11, 17 (bottom); Stuart Westmorland/Corbis, cover (background); Arvind Garg/Corbis, 4; Corel, 6, 7, 8, 9, 10, 12, 13, 14, 15, 16, 17 (top).

Project Manager: Rebecca Weber McEwen
Editor: Heidi Schoof
Photo Selectors: Rebecca Weber McEwen and Heidi Schoof
Designers: Jaime Martens and Les Tranby
Illustrator: Svetlana Zhurkina

Library of Congress Cataloging-in-Publication Data

Auch, Alison.
   Welcome to Brazil / by Alison Auch.
      p. cm. — (Spyglass books)
Summary: Briefly introduces life in modern-day Brazil.
Includes bibliographical references and index.
   ISBN 0-7565-0370-1 (hardcover)
   1. Brazil—Juvenile literature. 2. Brazil—Social life and
customs—Juvenile literature. [1. Brazil.] I. Title. II. Series.
   F2508.5 .A83 2002
   981—dc21
                           2002002749

Contents

Where Is Brazil?

Welcome to my country!
I live in Brazil.
I want to tell you
about my beautiful home.

Brazilian Flag

Did You Know?

Brazil is the largest
country in *South America.*

BRAZIL

PACIFIC
OCEAN

ATLANTIC
OCEAN

0   1,000 miles

0   1,000 km

N

W   E

S

At Home

My family lives in a small town.
Our houses are all white.
This helps keep them cool in the hot sun.

Some people travel along rivers to get to their houses.

At Work

Most people in Brazil
live near the ocean
or near a river.
My father catches fish
using a large net.
He sells these fish in town.

My brother works
in a small shop
like this one.

Let's Eat!

In Brazil, we eat
a lot of seafood.
My mom makes a special
Brazilian dish out of black
beans, beef, and pork.
I like to eat fresh fruit.

Bananas grow high in trees. They are picked when they are still green.

All Kinds of Clothes

We live near the ocean.
Here, the weather
is nice and warm.
In the mountains, it is cooler.
There, people need to wear
warm wool *ponchos*.

A white dress keeps this woman cool.
The scarf protects her head from
the hot sun.

Carnaval!

In Brazil, Carnaval is the biggest celebration of the year. I love the parades and music. People wear **costumes**.

During Carnaval, people dance in the streets.

Fun Facts

The Amazon river flows through Brazil. It is the biggest river in the world.

In Brazil, many people sleep in *hammocks* that hang above the floor.

The largest *rodent* in the world lives in Brazil. It is called a capybara.

Coffee is one of Brazil's main crops.

The Saci

In Brazil, there are many stories about a make-believe creature called the "saci."

The saci only has
one leg, and he wears
a magic red cap.

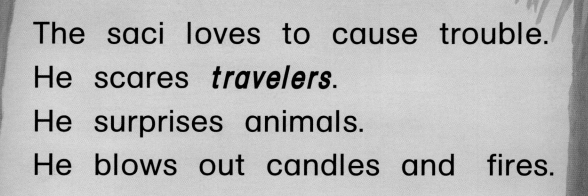

The saci loves to cause trouble.
He scares *travelers*.
He surprises animals.
He blows out candles and fires.

If you are ever in Brazil,
and something sneaks
up behind you...
watch out! It could
be the sneaky saci!

Glossary

costume–special clothing and makeup a person wears to dress up for celebrations and holidays

hammock–a hanging bed made from fabric or rope

poncho–a heavy piece of wool cloth that is pulled over the head and worn as a cape

rodent–a kind of four-legged animal, such as a mouse, with long teeth for gnawing

South America–one of the seven continents, or large areas of land found on Earth

traveler–a person who leaves home and visits different places

Learn More

Books

Dahl, Michael. *Brazil*. Mankato,
    Minn.: Bridgestone Books, 1997.
Petersen, David. *South America*.
    New York: Children's Press, 1998.
Thomson, Ruth. *The Rainforest People.*
    New York: Children's Press, 1996.

Web Site

www.ipl.org/youth/cquest
(click on "South & Central America,"
scroll to the "Brazil" section)

Index

GR: F
Word Count: 202

From Alison Auch

Reading and writing are my favorite things to do. When I'm not reading or writing, I like to go to the mountains or play with my little girl, Chloe.